Franz
SCHUBERT

Mass in G
D. 167

Vocal Score
Klavierauszug

SERENISSIMA MUSIC, INC.

CONTENTS

1. Kyrie – Andante con moto 3

2. Gloria – Allegro maestoso 9

3. Credo – Allegro moderato 16

4. Sanctus – Allegro maestoso 26

5. Benedictus – Andante grazioso 29

6. Agnus Dei – Lento 36

The alternative vocal parts (which appear in small notes), the optional wind and timpani parts were added by the composer's brother Ferdinand at the time of this work's first publication.

ORCHESTRA

2 Oboes, 2 Bassoons *(optional)*

2 Trumpets, Timpani *(optional)*

Organ

Violin I, Violin II, Viola, Violoncello, Double Bass

Duration: ca. 26 minutes

First performance: ca. March 7, 1815

Vienna

Complete orchestral parts compatible with this vocal score are available (Cat. No. A2716) from
E. F. Kalmus & Co., Inc.
6403 West Rogers Circle
Boca Raton, FL 33487 USA
(800) 434 - 6340
www.kalmus-music.com

Mass in G Major
D. 167

1. Kyrie

Franz Schubert
Piano reduction by Freidrich Spiro

2. Gloria

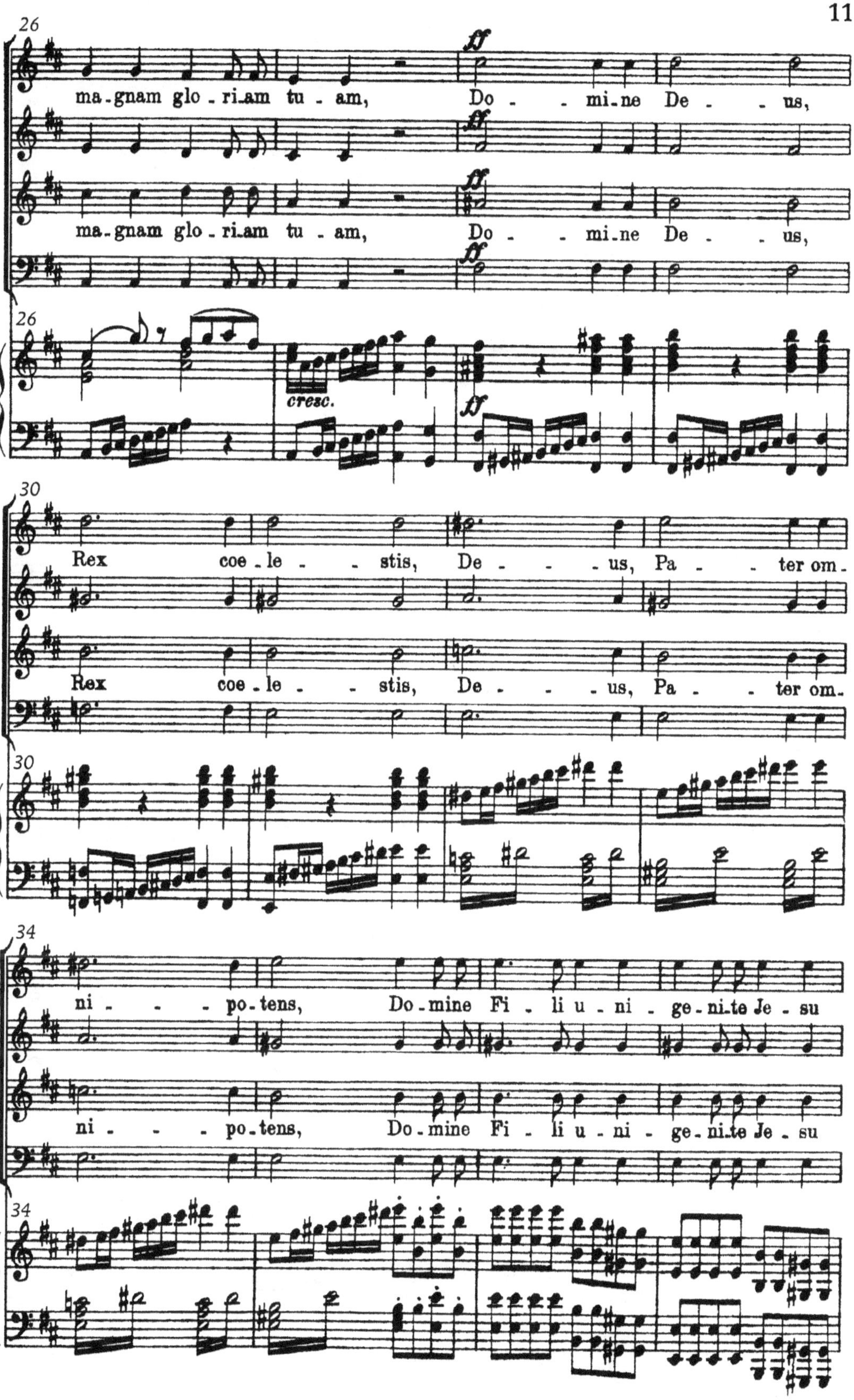
26
ff
ma-gnam glo-ri-am tu-am, Do - mi-ne De - - us,
ff
ff
ma-gnam glo-ri-am tu-am, Do - - mi-ne De - - us,
ff
26
cresc.
ff
30
Rex coe-le - - stis, De - - - us, Pa - - ter om-
Rex coe-le - - stis, De - - - us, Pa - - ter om-
30
34
ni - - - po-tens, Do-mine Fi - li u-ni - ge-ni-te Je-su
ni - - - po-tens, Do-mine Fi - li u-ni - ge-ni-te Je-su
34

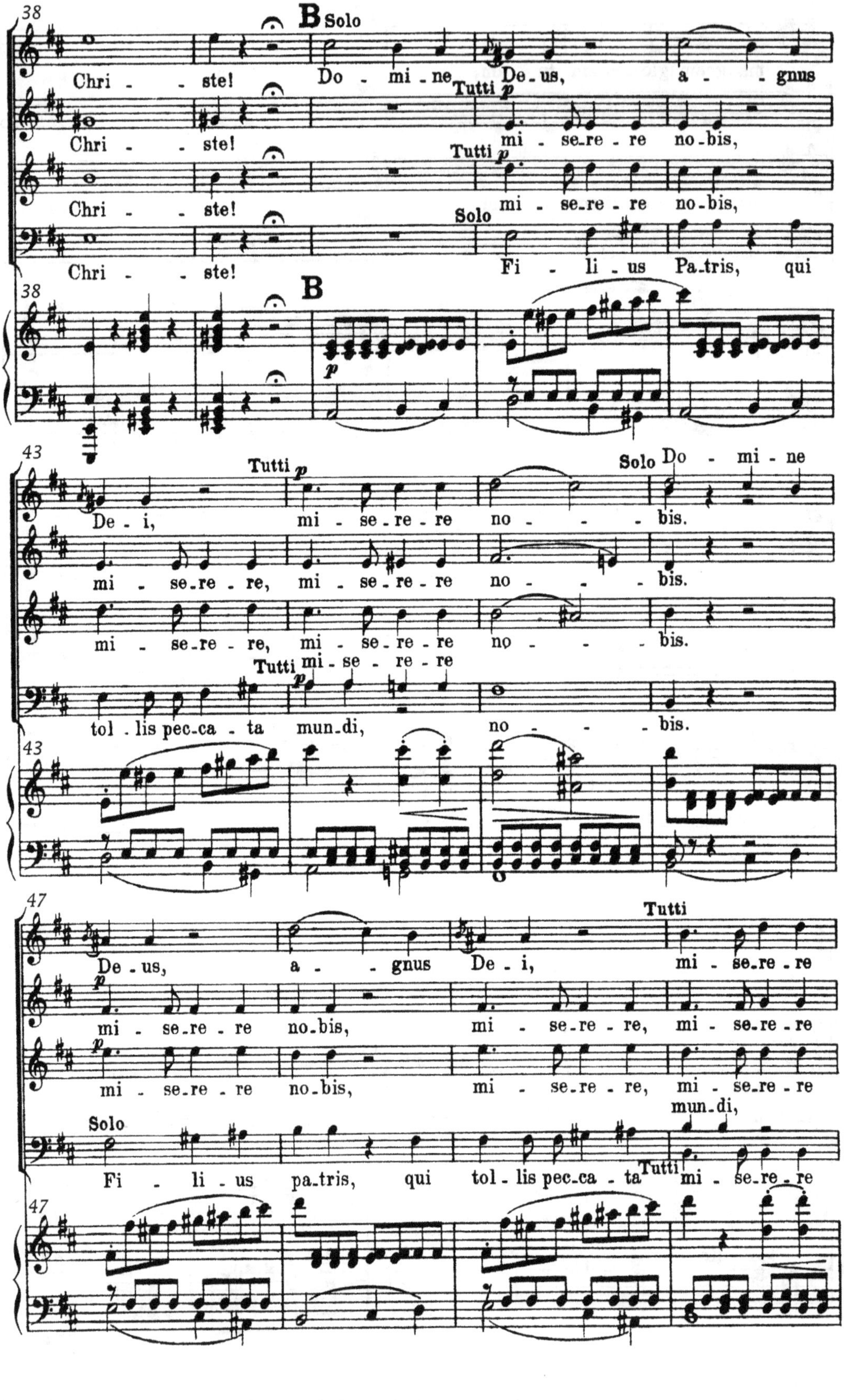
B
Solo
Tutti
Chri - ste! Do - mi - ne De - us, a - gnus
Chri - ste! mi - se - re - re no - bis,
Chri - ste! mi - se - re - re no - bis,
Chri - ste! Fi - li - us Pa - tris, qui
De - i, mi - se - re - re no - bis. Do - mi - ne
mi - se - re - re, mi - se - re - re no - bis.
mi - se - re - re, mi - se - re - re no - bis.
tol - lis pec - ca - ta mun - di, mi - se - re - re no - bis.
De - us, a - gnus De - i, mi - se - re - re
mi - se - re - re no - bis, mi - se - re - re, mi - se - re - re
mi - se - re - re no - bis, mi - se - re - re, mi - se - re - re
Fi - li - us pa - tris, qui tol - lis pec - ca - ta mun - di, mi - se - re - re

3. Credo

4. Sanctus

5. Benedictus

6. Agnus Dei

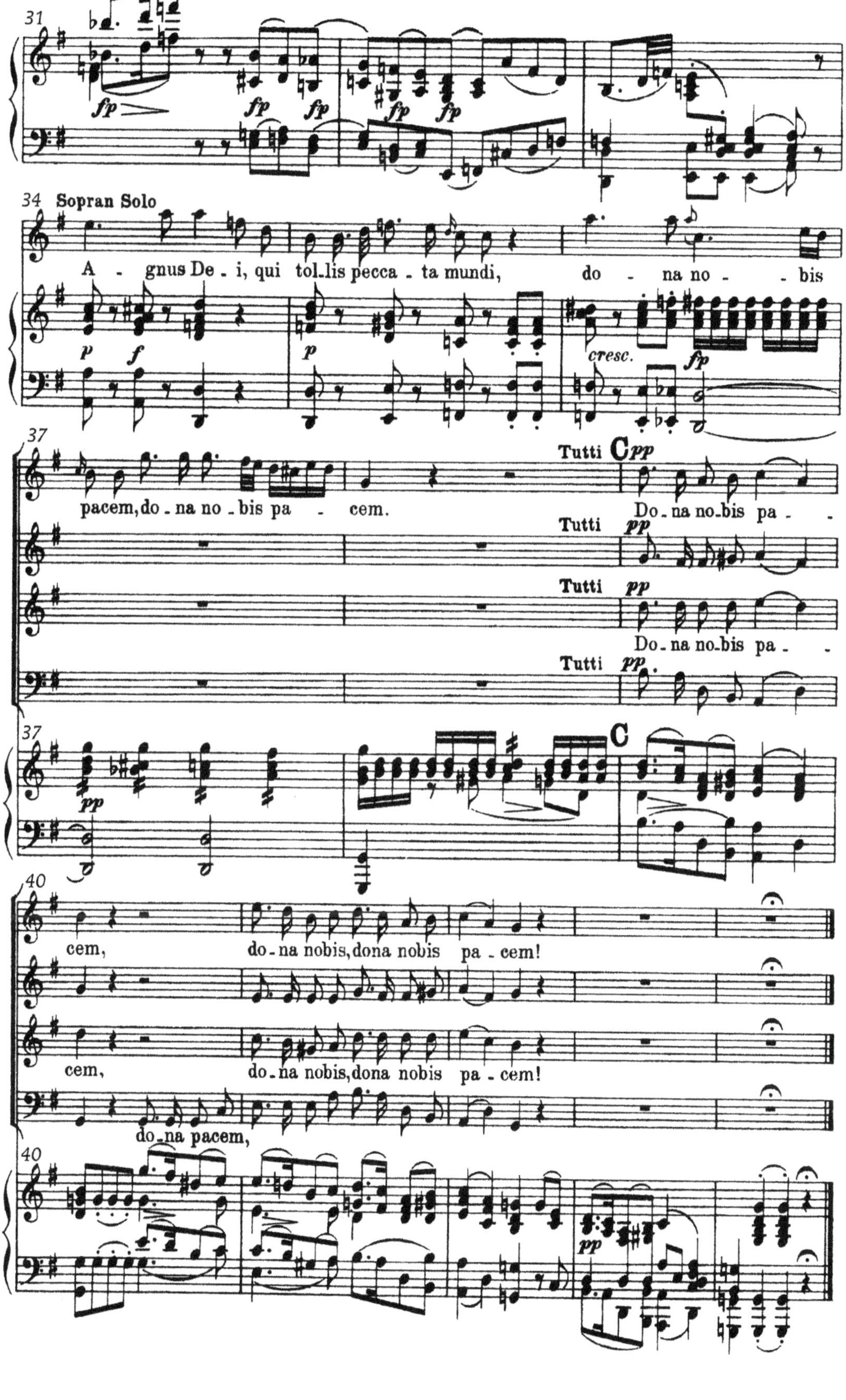
Sopran Solo
A - gnus De - i, qui tol - lis pecca - ta mundi, do - na no - - bis
pacem, do - na no - bis pa - cem.
Tutti
Do - na no - bis pa - - cem, do - na nobis, dona nobis pa - cem!
Do - na no - bis pa - - cem, do - na nobis, dona nobis pa - cem!
do - na pacem,
cresc.
C

www.ingramcontent.com/pod-product-compliance
Lightning Source LLC
Chambersburg PA
CBHW081025040426
42444CB00014B/3348